Patchwork called Life

Yamini Gupta

BookLeaf Publishing

India | USA | UK

Presentation by *BookLeaf Publishing*

Web: www.bookleafpub.com

E-mail: info@bookleafpub.com

ISBN: 9789363313163

First edition 2024

"To my family—my parents, siblings, and husband—who love and accept me for who I am, with all my superpowers, flaws and mistakes."

ACKNOWLEDGEMENT

"Thank you to Instagram for guiding me to BookLeaf Publishing and their inspiring 21-day poetry challenge.

A heartfelt thanks to the wonderful team at BookLeaf Publishing. Your engaging advertisements made it impossible for me to resist this challenge. This journey has allowed me to reflect and share parts of my life in ways I never imagined.

To you, the readers who choose this book, your engagement means the world to me. I invite you to weave your own experiences into these poems. Feel free to adapt, modify, and make them a part of your own narrative. It would bring me immense joy to see my words take on new life through your creativity.

And remember, you can choose to be beautiful and happy."

PREFACE

Life is like a quilt, made up of many different patches. Each patch represents a moment or experience that contributes to the whole. This book, *Patchwork Called Life*, is a collection of poems inspired by my own experiences and those I've witnessed in others. These poems capture the variety of life—the big and the small things we often overlook or take for granted.

In the rush of everyday life, it's easy to miss the small joys that brighten our days: a steaming hot cup of tea, morning blooms on your balcony or a hug from a loved one. I hope that these poems encourage you to pause and notice the beauty in the ordinary. Life is full of ups and downs, and it is these moments that shape who we are.

Each poem reflects on different aspects of life, from the simple pleasures we often ignore to the difficult times we must accept as part of our journey. It's important to celebrate life's joys and embrace the struggles, understanding that every experience is a piece of our personal story.

Through this collection, I want to share with you what I have learnt in all these years — that life, in all its complexity, is beautiful. It's the combination of all our experiences—both joyful and painful—that makes it worth celebrating. May these poems inspire you to cherish the little moments and find gratitude in the journey.

Thank you for joining me in this exploration of life's patchwork. I hope you find comfort, joy, and inspiration in these pages.

The Jade plant from my Balcony

Five years ago, in a brown bag,
It arrived in the month of May.
All frail, weak, and tiny,
With its leaves green and shiny.
The next day, I shifted it into a pot,
Since then, the jade has grown a lot.

It stays in the same spot every day,
Above the hibiscus, on my balcony,
Looking towards the sunlight,
Growing little by little, day and night.
It's become my darling, that tiny thing,
I love to watch it sing and swing.

It has seen it all, neglect and love,
Chatted with visitors, bees, and doves.
I would often look at it for hours,
And watch it dance in the rain showers.
Before I knew it, I became close to it,
Shared my life's troubles and grew thick.

One day I gave it a challenge,
To grow more and reach a certain height.
It started growing slowly, daily,

Grew a bit every day, my lovely.
Inch by inch, you became strong and tall,
With new and many shoots, against the wall.

From a tiny seedling, now all grown,
You are what I like to call my home.
Be it severe cold or a heat wave,
You lived through it all, how brave.
I left you behind, all alone,
You still thrived and outshone.

You taught me; keep yourself strong,
Never give up; from dusk to dawn.
Release the pain and hurt, the past is gone,
Focus on the future, where your dreams belong.
And remember to dance a little; smile and laugh,
Let the hopes be reborn as you move along.

Sounds from childhood

It happened a long time back,
When I could just relax, relax, relax,
Playing with my dolly all day
Chatting away; quack, quack, quack.
I laughed, I sang, and I danced around,
Enjoyed games of Tic-tac, sound after sound.

Mommy was my favourite,
She adored me so,
Her hugs were tight; hug, hug, hug,
She would never let me go.
Together we would sing, sing, sing,
Our voices blending, making joys ring.

I'd wait for papa eagerly,
Rushing to the door.
At the sound of the bell, ring, ring, ring,
Excited for what he had in store.
He brought me toys, an array so grand,
Filling our home with joy, quite as planned.

Soon came my sister, tiny and so sweet,
Her bright eyes sparkled, she was a treat.
From the moment I saw her, love did overflow,
As her proud big sister, I watched her grow.
For her, my heart held love, love, love,
She was our family's precious little dove.

Together we played, full of glee,
She'd mimic me keenly, all day, you see.
She'd look for me and shout, "Didi, Didi, Didi,"
In her eyes, I was the best, a sight to see.
When I made friends, she'd always tag along,
Singing 'My Didi is the best,' her favourite song.

A few years later, my brother made his entry,
Adorable and mischievous, adding to our sentry.
With sparkling eyes and a grin so wide,
He playfully nudged us to the side, side, side.
He quickly became the apple of everyone's eye,
Binding our family closer, ties reaching the sky.

From being an only child to the eldest of three,
The antics we'd pull were wild, wild, wild to see.
We were quite a handful, our parents often
complained,
Stubborn and loud, how we reigned and reigned.
We'd tussle and fight, but it was all in fun,
Sibling spats under the sun.

All the fights temporary; the love was real,
Strong for each other, with a great zeal.
We were one family, growing each new day,
No matter what anyone had to say, say, say.
These memories are the treasures of my story,
Adding to our family's glory, glory and glory.

The days of less

Gone are the days of childlike laughter,
Loud and carefree, rancour thereafter.
Parents would plead, "Keep the noise low,"
"Don't run wild, go slow."

Now I smile and laugh a bit less,
And think twice before showing distress.
This relentless pursuit of success
Brings luxuries and comforts, yet breeds stress.

Gone are the days so slow and so nice,
Mornings filled with dreams spun from night.
Now "fast, fast, fast" seems to fit just right,
As time and youth fade in this endless fight.

I miss those endless days of free time,
When sleeping in late was far from a crime.
Unaware of the corporate climb,
With friends, each moment was prime.

Back when shows were few, content was light,
One episode a week, that was our delight.
No social media, we cherished house invites,
Love built from presence, not followers or likes.

Those were the days of less and more,
Less to do; boredom often at the fore.
Social life was rich; not kept as a score;

We knew less and life had more in store.

I long to return to that life of less,
Fewer possessions; no need for excess.
A place where I'm the only one I need to impress,
Redefining what I would call a success.

In a world where no one cares how I dress or dine,
Where my life isn't judged online.
A life without this constant chase,
Where I can breathe, live at my own pace.

A cup of warmth

When the sky clears up at the dawn,
Time to wake up, the night is gone.
Living beings open their eyes and yawn,
Sipping tea as the new day is born.

Whether it's a day too long or slow,
Tea lifts your spirits when you're feeling low,
Dissolving problems, forging bonds, friend or foe,
Tea is timeless, the wise always know.

As the day progresses and burdens weigh heavy,
Ginger-brewed tea readies you for the levy,
To face challenges and things edgy,
With a steady energy, firm and savvy.

Add a pinch of cardamom for extra zest,
Savouring each moment, feeling truly blessed,
A sip of joy, life's sweet, cherished quest,
Gathering everyday joys, our hearts impressed.

When relations sour, jaggery sweetens the brew,
Transforming moods, a kindness anew,
Bitterness fades; warmth fills the view,
In every cup, tea's magic to pursue.

When your thoughts whirl, in a wild craze,
Add clove and fennel to soften the haze,

It grounds your mind, through complex mazes,
Restoring calm, for which you'll praise.

It's not just a beverage but a magical syrup,
Lifting spirits with every cup,
Giant worries or minor hiccups,
All seems well when tea fills your cup.

In the shade of Gulmohar

Six Gulmohar trees stand in a row,
When I step onto my balcony, they glow.
Near my current home, they grow and bloom,
Their fragrance wafting into my bedroom.

Every time I gaze at these Gulmohar trees,
I remember my childhood and its fond memories.
They also stood near my childhood home,
Where everyone loved me, and I was well-known.

Those were the carefree days of innocence,
When we dreamt and sang made-up songs with no
pretence.
I would play 'Ghar-Ghar'; I dreamed of my own
place,
Nothing fancy, just a peaceful space with grace.

In that dream house, there'd be a corner with a
bookshelf,
Where I could read, write, and reflect on myself.
Back then, my hopes were modest, my goals sincere,
To nurture a home and excel in roles held dear.

To be a loving mother, a devoted wife,
To enjoy every moment and build a joyful life.
These six Gulmohar trees remind me of the child in
me,
Who loved and conversed with every flower and tree.

That child was fearful, anxious about the future
unseen,
If only I knew then, how much cooler I'd have been.
That I wouldn't need a husband or a wife,
And would outshine expectations to everyone's
surprise.

These trees remind me of the times that have passed,
The days spent being shy, the shadows they cast.
They remind me of moments, both easy and tough,
Showing life is beautiful and colourful enough, even
when rough.

As days go by, times change, and seasons shift,
Life surprises you, offering its many gifts.
These Gulmohar trees link my new self with my old,
In their presence, I look forward to tomorrows, as life
unfolds.

Together in the city of dreams

I arrived there with bags and baggage,
To live in a new city, to manage my image.
Live with the one who is younger and wiser,
My sister, my confidante, my advisor.
We lived in Bombay, the first time together,
Collecting experiences, in all kinds of weather.

The first month, we settled in,
Navigating bus and cab routines.
The search continued for house help fine,
To clean, cook, and shape our life's design.
Step by step, we learned to create
A life within our gates, our own estate.

But Bombay life was harsh, unforgiving, tough,
House helps faltered, couldn't keep up enough.
They left, leaving our home in disarray,
Alone we stood, like yesterday's dismay.
The cleaning staff, their actions astray,
No one dared to point out or convey.

We often found ourselves in tough spots,
With neighbours insensitive, a nosy landlord, lots.
Navigating through, bitterness would rise,
In heated moments, tempers met the skies.
Still, through it all, my sister stood by me,

Like a solid rock, for everyone to see.

When we breathed a sigh and began to settle down,
Mumbai's rains poured in, the city began to drown.
Mould and moisture arrived as uninvited guests,
In these relentless trials, we found no rest.
While I retreated, overwhelmed by the invasion,
My sister stepped up, mastered the occasion.

She became my guide when I felt low,
Cheering me up, urging me to let things go.
Whenever worries clouded my view, we'd walk,
She'd clear my mind with her uplifting talk.
Slowly, with her, Mumbai became my home,
As long as she's here, I'll never be alone.

With her around, Mumbai looked beautiful,
I began to heal; my heart became full.
Be it the generous sea or the city's glamour and
glitter,
This all is giving and gorgeous, just like my sister.
She is my anchor, my hope, my pride,
In her is where all my strength resides.

Four Seasons of Love

O' my darling, my love is true,
For all the days we spent together,
And the nights I spent without you.
My soul pines for your presence,
How much? I wish you knew.
My dreams are yours, old and new.

I spend my days in longing,
Waiting for Spring to arrive,
When flowers bloom
And songs of love revive.
When fortune swings,
I'll accept whatever it brings.

500 days of being apart,
Longing to be together.
Love is the only reality,
Come what may, whatever.
Through four seasons, in all weather,
I am yours, forever.

When summer came knocking,
I knew you would be around.
Holding my hand, by my side,
Listening to my soul's sounds.

You are my every desire,
In you, all heavens are found.

The rains felt like your embrace,
Like when you kissed my face.
The breeze touched me gently,
As you did in those cherished days.
Come soon, I wait for you
With all my heart and soul in a daze.

Unequal or Unique

Each displays different colours and hues,
Some red and orange, others in blues.
Every bloom is unique, it's true,
Together in the same garden, they grew.

Some scented more, some shone so bright,
Choosing one over another just isn't right.
Nature shows no favour, gives equal light,
Together, they form a stunning sight.

One day a bloom was favoured more,
Adored by visitors like never before.
The gardener nurtured it more and more,
Leaving the rest alone, ignored and sore.

With adulation, it filled with pride,
Behaviour altered, it scorned and did chide.
It sowed division, creating a wide divide,
Some blooms preferred, others set aside.

This continued until a stormy day,
Rains thundered down, leading many astray.
Damage was high, no one could shy away,
Hard times spared none in their fray.

Labels are superficial, the bloom now understood,
Dropped all pretence, along with falsehood.
Rankings do not define who is good,
We are unique and special, as we should.

Untold Classroom Stories

There were many students in one class,
Three were more sincere, first in every task.
The teacher favoured a few over the rest,
Giving special treatment to two, neglecting the best.
The last one felt low, unseen, and demeaned,
Feeling unimportant and un-esteemed.

The two received smiles, claps, and stars on their
books,
While the third, in the corner, was met with
overlooked looks.
She mimicked their handwriting and their
mannerisms,
Hoping to garner the same enthusiastic favouritism.
But the teacher's eyes never seemed to glance her
way,
Leaving her with self-doubt, untamed and in disarray.

The third one tried befriending the favoured pair,
Learning how the teacher's affections ensnare.
She attempted to join their circle, to become one of
them,
Yet the more she tried, the more she felt condemned.
Felt like an outsider, an alien, left to reside,
It troubled her deeply, this pain she couldn't hide.

At thirteen, she noticed life's harsh disparities,
Struggled with confidence, umpteen insecurities

She matured into someone with love and kindness,
Transformed by the pain and the world's unfairness.
The injustices she witnessed stirred deep compassion,
Motivating her to help others in her own fashion.

She learned to assert herself and to challenge wrong,
Yet beneath her bravery, the hurt remained strong.
Unaware of why her heart felt pain so acutely,
Whenever faced with words unjust and unduly.
Healing came through love, and time taught
forgiveness,
She embraced life's joys, found peace in kindness.

The Scars of Society

Ever known the feeling of a fluttering heart,
With butterflies dancing, playing their part?
When you see him, so dashing and smart,
You long to be close, never to be apart.

One such person entered her life,
Asking for pens and pencils, sparking a rife.
His voice was addictive, his presence a delight,
She fell for him, lost in love's flight.

School meetings were brief, never enough,
Their talks cut short, interactions tough.
He started showing near her cherished home,
Stealing glances, in her view he'd roam.

She'd stand on her balcony, he'd stay near,
Leaving letters that she cherished dear.
A platonic bond, pure, undefined,
Two teenagers, their closeness intertwined.

Yet, unseen by them, clear to all around,
Neighbours whispered, their disdain unbound.
She felt the shift, the coldness of their whispering,
A pain so deep, her heart persistently blistering.

The elders rolled their eyes, her peers began to
ostracise,
Alone she stood, her fears masked by a clever guise.

She noted every glance, each laugh that passed her
by,
Each one a sharp reminder, making her question why.

That boycott cut her deep, planting seeds of doubt,
Fear and anxiety within her as depression took its
route.
Behind her back they whispered, with laughter cruel
and sharp,
Facing her they scorned, branding her a mark.

What started at just fourteen,
Persisted and haunted her at seventeen and nineteen.
Old tales were retold as she transitioned to new,
With each retelling, the rumours took a fresher hue.

She became a subject of gossip, a source of idle
thrills,
While they spun tales, she grew talents and envious
skills.
As stories spread and the gossip mill fiercely turned,
She forged ahead, from her past she had learned.

No one paused to think, how would the child feel?
She carried the trauma well into her adult life's reel.
She grew up, found love, carved a niche in society,
Yet deep within, battled fear, stress, and anxiety.

We all carry demons, hidden scars inside,
A little love and kindness can turn the tide.
A helping hand, a warm hug and a smile so bright,
Can mend a soul, bring darkness to light.

Stolen Summers

I was a child, barely ten,
It happened around then.
Amidst my extended family,
Who claimed to protect me fully.

I had gone to spend my summer vacation
Away from my parents, with blood relations.
All I sought was love and validation,
But returned all grown up, a shadowed
transformation.

I asked my cousin if he wanted to play,
He buried his nose in books and walked away.
But then he returned later that same day,
"Will teach you a new kind of game," he would say.

I was just a child; agreed to join in,
Thinking I'd share with my friends and might win.
"I won't tell anyone," he made me promise to him,
And then began the episode, far too grim.

It was all a secret and a thing too hushed,
He said it was not wrong; no need to make a fuss.
But it felt awkward; it felt strange and bad,
I could do nothing to make it stop; too sad.

It happened a few times during that trip
Whenever he would find me alone, he would unzip
He would ask me to touch and do things
It was just a game; what wrong it could bring

A week or ten days later, I went back home,
I told nobody; the secret remains my own.
Life went on; from a child, I became all grown,
The wounds it left, the scars still shown.

What a child hides inside; you might not know,
If they are hurting or in pain; they might not show.
Behind their smiles, there could be fears that never
go,
Before they could be a child, they were forced to
grow.

You might not be able to fix their past,
Or heal the wounds that forever last.
But you can offer love that's unconditional and vast,
And be the comfort that helps them surpass.

LOVE YOURSELF

Me above YOU!

I stepped up for myself,
Found myself a standing ground.
I became my own friend
When there was no one around.

I loved myself in despair,
And cried myself to sleep.
Either way, I never gave up;
I continued to take the leap.

I refused to give up then,
I won't do it even now.
No matter what you do or say,
I will choose myself over you.

Every time you let go of me,
And silently disappear,
I find the inner strength
That existed but I wasn't aware.

When you treat me wrong
And think less of me,
I love myself a lot more,
For you and the world to see.

You leave me behind,
You lie and you cheat,
I don't blame myself anymore,

Instead, I remain upbeat.

I realised: chaos is outside,
And the noise is within.
When I choose me above you,
I win, I win, I win.

Whispers of Hope

She was stunningly beautiful,
Soft-spoken, gentle, and ever so graceful.
Wherever she went, she captured all eyes,
Onlookers' hearts skipped beats as she passed by.
Her smile and laughter made her eyes gleam,
To many, she seemed an unreachable dream.

She was loved by friends and family alike,
She never did a thing to be disliked.
Every box checked, each step was right,
Like a fairy tale, she was pure delight.
She brought hope so bright,
A soothing sight for hearts and eyes.

One day she was found in the midst of a mess,
People questioned, adding to her stress.
She had never felt such high duress,
When repeatedly pressured, she confessed.
Admitting she had made mistakes, erred a bit,
"How could you?" they cried, throwing a fit.

Her friends turned away, left her to stand alone,
Family ties severed, as though she was disowned.
"Was my error so colossal?" she often wondered,
Faced with humiliation and shame unnumbered.
Linked to rumours wherever she roamed,
She became the butt of jokes, sadly intoned.

Overwhelmed by rejection so harsh and keen,
She sought a final escape, unseen.
"Better to end it all at once," she mused,
To flee the shame that had her confused.
One quiet afternoon, her decision was made,
Resolved to end her life's painful charade.

She clasped a sharp-edged knife, tight,
Wrist forward, poised for a quick, decisive slice.
Summoning courage with all her might,
Ready to end the struggle, to stop the fight.
Just then, her mom embraced her from behind,
Whispering softly, "Everything will be all right."

Her little sister came, took her hand with speed,
Showered her with love, stood firm in need.
"What will become of them if I'm gone?"
This thought struck hard; it finally dawned.
Setting fear aside, she rose with newfound might,
"Through kindness, we win; through kindness, we
ignite."

Shame is not the answer, humiliation's not a must,
Resolve each situation with peace; in kindness, trust.
If you see someone struggling, reach for their hand,
Offer them love, and try to understand.
Today it's them, feeling alone and unloved,
Imagine if it were someone you cherished and loved.

Guided by Grace

When the chips are down,
And life delivers blow after blow,
Don't you dare give up, no—
Pick yourself up, stand and show.
Through paths that remain unknown,
God helps—you're not alone.
She constantly watches over you,
Even when you can't see through.

Remember the stranger who showed up in a strange
land,
When you were being mobbed, he lent a helping
hand.
He intervened, shooed them away,
Just appeared, strong and calm in his way.
You wondered from where he came and why,
Softly murmuring, 'What a nice guy.'
Who was he, if not God in disguise?
Came to help, so you weren't lost to the skies.

Don't ever feel you are lonely or alone,
God takes care; you're never on your own.
Lifting you up, she sends you joys,
Those lucky surprises you truly enjoy.
A best friend found when in need,
Wiping your tears, showing the lead.
Life's sorrows and disappointments are her tests,
To hone your spirit, from better to best.

When you believed it was doomsday,
She became the friend who would stay.
In that darkness, a shining ray,
Paving the path; showing you the way.
She fought with hundreds by your side,
In those moments, your strength and guide.
A friend, inspired by the divine,
Believe in yourself, you are meant to shine.

Don't fear life's difficulties or setbacks,
In the grand scheme, these are just knick-knacks.
With heart pure and will so strong,
You'll scale mountains, just keep treading along.
When things get tough and you're at your wit's end,
Don't panic, she'll send help to hand.
From her, we came and to her, we'll merge,
She is the cosmic energy, where all things converge.

Journey into Joy

Take that break
Don't just wait
Plan, then fly
Reach the sky

Climb high peaks
Walk through rains
Explore unknown paths
Feel foreign winds

Sit by sea
Venture out far
Bask in sun
Chase the horizon

Dive into waves
Savour each meal
Laugh heartily, often
Embrace perfect flaws

Stroll long paths
Share quiet talks
Smile even more
Treasure every moment

You will heal
Breathing cool breeze
That whispers secrets

From distant seas

Hug ancient trees
Converse with bees
Observe flowers bloom
Gleefully, without gloom

Seek silent moments
Embrace sweet solitude
Celebrate life's gifts
With joyful gratitude

Travel far, wide
Rest, or explore
Pray, play, discover
Anywhere you adore.

Reclaim Yourself

Does the world often leave you troubled,
Feeling bruised; your pain doubled.
It's tough and cruel, it won't soften,
With rejections and betrayals not forgotten.
So you've learned to move with caution,
Bitter and sore, with few other options.

Others' opinions seem to weigh you down,
Their actions unkind, making you frown.
You crave their love, seek their validation,
Dancing to their tune, lost in that equation.
Exhausted, drained from playing their game,
Changing daily, you're never quite the same.

Slowly, you'll begin to realise
That chaos reigns beyond these skies.
Lead from within, stand up and rise;
This is the path walked by the wise.
Channel all your energy, let it mobilise;
Remember, you're the ultimate prize.

Trust your gut and instincts true,
Derive energy from within, as the wise do.
Forgive and forget what others say,
Let your intellect show you the way.
You are the one who matters the most,
Live from within, be your own host.

Invest in yourself, strengthen your inner power,
Remind yourself you matter, every single hour.
Take long walks, enjoy restorative showers,
Spend time in nature, treat yourself to flowers.
Cut out the excess, silence all the noise,
Embrace this daily; discover deeper joys.

Life is beautiful, you will realise,
Don't waste it on worry or compromise.
Focus on love and live for today,
Your wishes matter, come what may.
Others' opinions? They are inconsequential,
You're the star, the real deal, that is essential.

YOU ARE ENOUGH

Finding Strength Within

When they leave you behind,
Or you feel terribly resigned
In those moments, centre your mind
To yourself, be incredibly kind.

In moments of rejection
or when kins abandon
Love yourself a bit more
Connect with nature; outdoors.

You are your own hero,
Watch yourself grow.
Don't rush, take it slow,
Let your brilliance show.

Speak your truth,
Raise your cup.
Toast yourself saying,
"I am enough."

Declare, 'I love myself,'
Let your light shine,
O' my lovely,
You'll do just fine.

Forge your path,
Chart your course.
You are a force,

Your own power source.

You are the boss,
You are in control,
With each step,
You will reach your goal.

Believe in your worth,
Let it endorse,
For in loving yourself,
You will find your force.

hope

One day, it all works out

She keeps going on,
avoiding signs of burnout.
Is it even worth it?
She sometimes doubts.
She had read somewhere that
one day, it will all work out.

She grew up with less and none,
Searched for a confidante, just one.
Many came and many left,
Leaving her scarred and stressed.
But she remained on the lookout,
With whom, it would all work out.

Her childhood was rough,
And teenage years even tougher.
Only when she became an adult,
Did she realise she doesn't have to suffer.
Every day she picks up her battered self,
Braving through the day with or without help.

But the past continues to linger on,
It hurts; pulls her back.
Every day she feels like giving up,
But then she doesn't.
She makes it through one more time,
And waits for her share of sunshine.

People judge her; give her labels,
She ignores; no longer cares much.
They often make her feel unseen,
Seed her with low self-esteem.
She goes on; goes out and about,
Because one day it all works out!

At the end, she paused and thought about
Her life and if all of it really made sense.
Lo and behold, it looked lovely,
A work of art, her own beautiful mess.
It was life, imperfect and unforgiving throughout,
But indeed, everything almost always worked out.

www.ingramcontent.com/pod-product-compliance
Lightning Source LLC
LaVergne TN
LVHW041227200726

843507LV00013B/2602